The Teacher

By Jenny Giles
Photographs by Lindsay Edwards

I am at school
with my friends.

We are going
to see our teacher.

We go into the classroom,

and our teacher smiles at us.

We help her with the books.

In the morning,

we have our news time.

Our teacher talks to us,

and we talk to her.

She writes a story with us,

and we read it with her.

Today is Friday.

It is a sunny day.
We went for a walk
to look at the trees
by our classroom.

Some of the trees
have new green leaves.

I read my book to the teacher.

The teacher reads a story to us.

At playtime,

we go outside.

We run and play games,

and our teacher looks after us.

After play,

we run into the classroom.

Our teacher is not pleased,

and she stops us.

She says that someone will get hurt

if we run inside.

She makes us walk.

We do maths at school.

The teacher helps us

with our work.

I am good at maths.

15

After school, Mum comes to get me.

I wave to my teacher, and I go home.

NELSON
A Cengage Company

The Teacher

Text: Jenny Giles
Series consultant: Annette Smith
Publishing editor: Simone Calderwood
Editor: Ted Carisbrooke
Project editor: Annabel Smith
Series design: James Lowe
Design: James Lowe and Karen Mayo
Photographs: Lindsay Edwards
Production controllers: Emily Moore and Emma Roberts
Reprint: Siew Han Ong

Acknowledgements

Back cover (background pattern): Shutterstock.com/sahua d.

Cengage Learning would like to thank Banyule Primary School for their assistance with this book.

First edition published in 1998

PM Guided Reading
Blue Levels 11/12

Our Parents
The Teacher
The Doctor
The Dentist
The Optometrist
The Vet

Text © 2017 The Estate of Jenny Giles
Photographs © 2017 Cengage Learning Australia Pty Limited

ISBN 978 0 17 039490 1

Cengage Learning Australia
Level 7, 80 Dorcas Street
South Melbourne, Victoria Australia 3205
Phone: 1300 790 853

Cengage Learning New Zealand
Unit 4B Rosedale Office Park
331 Rosedale Road, Albany, North Shore NZ 0632
Phone: 0800 449 725

For learning solutions, visit **cengage.com.au**

Printed in China by 1010 Printing International Ltd
4 5 6 7 21

PM

1
2
3
4
5
6
7
8
9
10
11
12
13
14

Non-fiction

ISBN-13: 978-0170394901

L 11

L 12

NELSON
A Cengage Company

9 780170 394901